Adapted Reading and Study Workbook

Earth's Waters

PRENTICE HALL Science Explorer

PEARSON

Prentice Hall

Boston, Massachusetts
Upper Saddle River, New Jersey

ISBN 13: 978-0-328-71801-6
ISBN 10:   0-328-71801-7

1 2 3 4 5 6 7 8 9 10 V011 15 14 13 12 11

Earth's Waters

Chapter 1 Earth: The Water Planet

Chapter 2 Freshwater Resources

Chapter 3 Ocean Motions

Chapter 4 Ocean Zones

Earth: The Water Planet

The Properties of Water (pages 6–11)

The Structure of Water (page 7)

Key Concept: **The positive hydrogen ends of one water molecule attract the negative oxygen ends of nearby water molecules. As a result, the water molecules tend to stick together.**

- Atoms join together to form molecules. A water molecule is made up of two hydrogen atoms attached to an oxygen atom.

- Water is made up of polar water molecules. A **polar molecule** has electrically charged areas. The oxygen end of a water molecule has a negative charge. The hydrogen ends each have a positive charge.

- Polar molecules are like magnets. In magnets, opposite poles attract each other. In polar molecules, atoms with opposite charges attract each other.

Answer the following questions. Use your textbook and the ideas above.

1. A molecule that has electrically charged areas is

   called a(an) _____ molecule.

2. Circle the letter of each sentence that is true about the structure of water.
   a. Water is made up of polar water molecules.
   b. A water molecule contains two hydrogen atoms.
   c. A water molecule contains two oxygen atoms.

Earth: The Water Planet

3. The picture below shows a water molecule. Circle the part of the molecule that has a slight negative charge.

Hydrogen atom

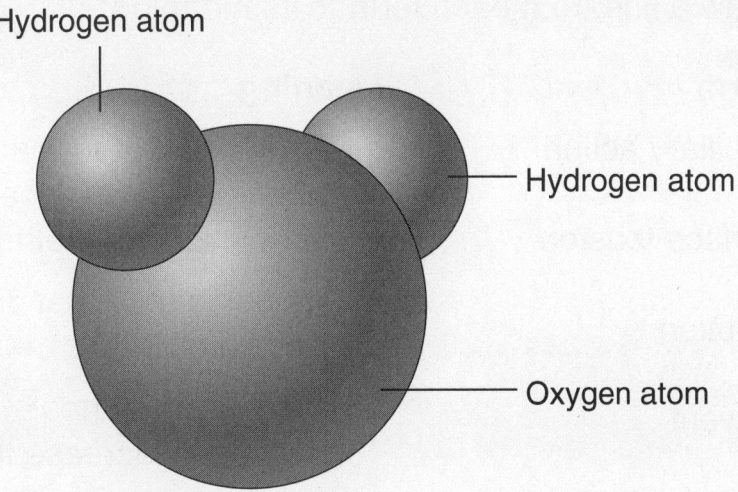

Hydrogen atom

Oxygen atom

Key Properties of Water (pages 8–9)

Key Concept: **The properties of water include capillary action, surface tension, the ability to dissolve many substances, and high specific heat.**

- **Capillary action** is the combined attraction among water molecules and between water molecules and other molecules. One result of capillary action is that water rises in a tube.

- **Surface tension** is the tightness across the surface of water. Some insects can even walk across water because surface tension keeps them from sinking.

- Many substances dissolve in water. A **solution** is a mixture that forms when one substance dissolves in another. The substance that does the dissolving is called a **solvent**. Because so many substances dissolve into water, water is called the "universal solvent."

- **Specific heat** is the amount of heat needed to increase the temperature of a substance by 1°C. Different substances have different specific heats. Water needs a lot of heat to increase its temperature—water has a very high specific heat.

Name _____ Date _____ Class _____

Earth: The Water Planet

Answer the following question. Use your textbook and the ideas on page 5.

4. Draw a line from each term to its meaning.

Term	Meaning
capillary action	**a.** a mixture that forms when one substance dissolves into another
surface tension	
solution	**b.** the substance that does the dissolving
solvent	**c.** the amount of heat needed to increase the temperature of a substance by 1°C
specific heat	**d.** the combined attraction among water molecules and between water molecules and other molecules
	e. the tightness across the surface of water

Changing State (pages 10–11)

Key Concept: **Ice is solid water, the familiar form of water is a liquid, and the water vapor in the air is a gas.**

• Water is the only substance on Earth that commonly exists in all three different states of matter—as a gas, a liquid, and a solid.

• Liquid water can become a gas when it is boiled. It can also become a gas by evaporation. **Evaporation** is when molecules at the surface of a liquid change into a gas.

Earth: The Water Planet

- The way a gas changes into a liquid is called **condensation.** When you fog up a window by breathing on it, you see the effects of condensation.

- When water freezes, water changes from a liquid to a solid. When ice melts, water changes from a solid to a liquid.

Answer the following questions. Use your textbook and the ideas on page 6 and above.

5. Read each word in the box. In each sentence below, fill in the correct word.

| evaporation | precipitation | condensation |

   a. The process by which a gas changes into a liquid is called _____.

   b. The process by which molecules at the surface of a liquid change into a gas is called

   _____.

6. Complete the table about how water changes state.

How Water Changes State		
Type of Change	**Starting State**	**Ending State**
Melting	solid	liquid
Boiling	**a.** _____	gas
Evaporation	liquid	**b.** _____
Condensation	**c.** _____	liquid
Freezing	liquid	**d.** _____

Earth: The Water Planet

Water on Earth (pages 12–17)

All Living Things Need Water (page 13)

Key Concept: **All living things need water in order to carry out their body processes. In addition, many living things use water for shelter.**

- Water makes up nearly two thirds of your body. You need water to live. All other living things also need water to live.

- Plants need water to carry out photosynthesis. **Photosynthesis** (foh toh SIN thuh sis) is how plants make their own food.

- Water provides habitats for many living things. A **habitat** is where an organism lives and can get all the things it needs.

Answer the following questions. Use your textbook and the ideas above.

1. Read each word in the box. In each sentence below, fill in the correct word.

condensation	photosynthesis	habitat

   a. Where an organism lives and can get all the things it needs is a _____.
   b. The process by which plants make their own food is called _____.

2. Is the following sentence true or false? Water is not necessary for most living things to live. _____

Earth: The Water Planet

Distribution of Earth's Water (pages 14–15)

Key Concept: **Most of Earth's water—roughly 97 percent—is salt water found in oceans. Only 3 percent is fresh water.**

• Earth's oceans include the Atlantic Ocean, the Pacific Ocean, and the Indian Ocean. Together, the oceans cover a larger area than all the land on Earth combined.

• Oceans hold most of Earth's water. The water in oceans is salt water.

• About three quarters of Earth's fresh water is in huge ice masses near the North and South poles. There are also floating chunks of ice called icebergs.

• About a quarter of Earth's fresh water is groundwater. **Groundwater** fills the cracks and spaces in underground soil and rock.

• Rivers and lakes contain fresh water.

Answer the following questions. Use your textbook and the ideas above.

3. The circle graph below shows the distribution of Earth's water. Circle the letter of the part of Earth's water that is only 3 percent.

   a. salt water   **b.** fresh water   **c.** groundwater

Distribution of Water on Earth

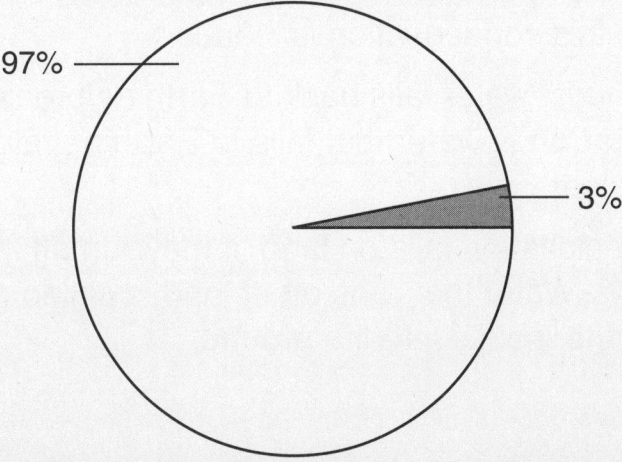

Earth: The Water Planet

4. The water that fills the cracks and spaces in underground soil and rock is called

   _____.

5. Circle the letter of each sentence that is true about the distribution of Earth's water.

   a. About a quarter of Earth's fresh water is groundwater.

   b. Rivers and lakes contain salt water.

   c. The oceans cover a larger area than all the land on Earth combined.

The Water Cycle (pages 16–17)

Key Concept: **In the water cycle, water moves from bodies of water, land, and living things on Earth's surface to the atmosphere and back to Earth's surface.**

- The **water cycle** is how water moves from Earth's surface to the atmosphere and back again. The water cycle never stops. It has no beginning or end.

- The sun is the source of energy for the water cycle.

- Water evaporates from Earth's surface. Water is always evaporating from oceans and lakes. Water is given off by plants as water vapor in a process called **transpiration**.

- When water vapor in the air cools, it condenses. The result of this condensation is clouds.

- From clouds, water falls back to Earth as precipitation. **Precipitation** is water that falls to Earth as rain, snow, hail, or sleet.

- If the precipitation falls on land, if may run off into rivers and lakes. Water that runs off of land is called runoff. Some water soaks into the ground.

Earth: The Water Planet

Answer the following questions. Use your textbook and the ideas on page 10.

6. The process by which water moves from Earth's surface to the atmosphere and back again is the

_____.

7. Read each word in the box. In each sentence below, fill in the correct word.

| transpiration | precipitation | condensation |

   a. Water that falls to Earth as rain, snow, hail, or

      sleet is called _____.

   b. The process in which water is given off by plants as

      water vapor is called _____.

8. Circle the letter of each sentence that is true about the water cycle.

   a. The water cycle begins with the formation of clouds.

   b. The result of the condensation in the air is clouds.

   c. The sun is the energy source for the water cycle.

Earth: The Water Planet

Surface Water (pages 19–27)

River Systems (pages 20–21)

Key Concept: **A river and all its tributaries together make up a river system.**

- All fresh water comes from precipitation. Fresh water on Earth may be moving, as in streams and rivers. Or, it may be still, as in ponds and lakes.

- **Tributaries** are the streams and small rivers that flow into a big river.

- The land area that supplies water to a river system is called a **watershed**. A river drains a region. The watershed of the Mississippi River covers nearly one third of the United States.

- A **divide** is a ridge of land that separates one watershed from another watershed. Streams on each side of a divide flow in different directions.

Answer the following questions. Use your textbook and the ideas above.

1. Draw a line from each term to its meaning.

Term	Meaning
tributary	**a.** the land area that supplies water to a river system
watershed	**b.** a ridge of land that separates one watershed from another
divide	
	c. a small river that flows into a big river

Earth: The Water Planet

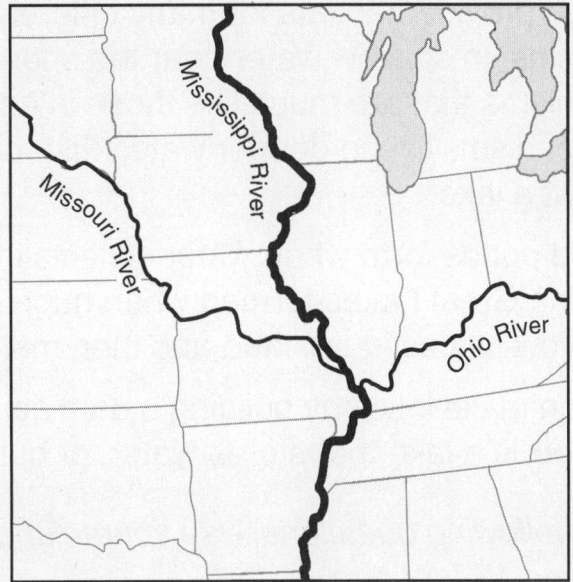

2. The map above shows part of a river system. Circle the letter of each river that is a tributary.
   a. Missouri River
   b. Mississippi River
   c. Ohio River

3. Is the following sentence true or false? All fresh water comes from precipitation. _____

Ponds and Lakes (pages 22–25)

Key Concept: **Ponds and lakes form when water collects in hollows and low-lying areas of land.**

• Ponds and lakes are bodies of fresh water. They contain still water, which is also called standing water.

• Ponds and lakes get their water from rain, from melting snow, and from runoff. Some ponds and lakes get their water from rivers or from groundwater.

• Many different kinds of organisms find habitats in ponds. Plants grow throughout a pond. Plantlike organisms called algae also live in ponds.

- Lakes also provide habitats for many different kinds of organisms. In shallow water near the shore, a lake has organisms that are much like those in a pond. Fewer organisms live in deeper water. Fish can live throughout a lake.

- Lakes and ponds form when water collects in low areas of land. The Great Lakes formed when huge glaciers made hollow places in the land and then melted.

- People can make lakes by building a dam across a river. A **reservoir** is a lake that stores water for human use.

Answer the following questions. Use your textbook and the ideas on page 13 and above.

4. Circle the letter of each sentence that is true about ponds and lakes.

   a. People can make lakes by building a dam across a river.

   b. Lakes provide habitats for many different kinds of organisms.

   c. Some ponds and lakes get their water from groundwater.

5. A lake that stores water for human use is a(an)

   _____.

How Lakes Can Change (pages 26–27)

Key Concept: In addition to seasonal changes, a lake can undergo long-term changes that may eventually lead to its death.

- Lakes change as the seasons change. For example, the water is warmer in summer than in winter.

Earth: The Water Planet

- Temperature differences through a year cause water to sink and rise in lakes. This mixes the water and spreads nutrients through a lake. **Nutrients** are substances that plants and algae need to grow.

- A lake may change over a long period of time because of eutrophication. **Eutrophication** (yoo troh fih KAY shun) is the build up of nutrients in a lake.

- The buildup of nutrients causes algae to grow over the surface of a lake. Plants under the algae die. Animals that depend on the plants for food also die. Dead material fills up the lake, making it shallower. After a time, the lake dies, and a grassy field takes over.

- Sometimes lakes and ponds die because a river or stream that provides water dries up.

Answer the following questions. Use your textbook and the ideas on page 14 and above.

6. Read each word in the box. In each sentence below, fill in the correct word.

eutrophication	nutrient	habitat

   a. The build up of nutrients in a lake is called

   _____.

   b. A substance that plants and algae need to grow

   is a(an) _____.

7. Circle the letter of each sentence that is true about how lakes can change.

   a. Sometimes a lake dies because a river that provides water dries up.

   b. Lakes change as the seasons change.

   c. The buildup of nutrients in a lake causes algae to grow over the surface of the lake.

Earth: The Water Planet

Wetland Environments (pages 28–33)

Types of Wetlands (page 29)

Key Concept: **The three common types of freshwater wetlands are marshes, swamps, and bogs.**

- A **wetland** is a land area that is covered with water during at least part of the year. Some wetlands are covered with water all year round.

- Marshes are grassy areas covered by shallow water or a stream. Cattails and other tall plants grow in marshes.

- Swamps look like flooded forests. Swamps have trees and shrubs growing in the water. Swamps are common in warm and wet climates.

- Bogs have acidic water. Mosses grow in bogs. Bogs are common in cooler areas.

Answer the following questions. Use your textbook and the ideas above.

1. A land area that is covered with shallow water during at least part of the year is a(an) _____.

2. Circle the letter of each sentence that is true about wetlands.
   a. Bogs are common in warmer areas.
   b. There is only one common type of freshwater wetland.
   c. Some wetlands are covered with water all year round.

3. The picture above shows one type of wetland. Circle the letter of the type of wetland shown in the picture.

   a. marsh

   b. swamp

   c. bog

The Everglades: A Wetland (pages 30–31)

Key Concept: **Agriculture, development, and the introduction of new species are some human activities that threaten the Florida Everglades.**

- The Everglades in southern Florida is a special region of wetlands. Everglades National Park covers part of the Everglades.

- In the Everglades, a wide, shallow stream of water flows over the land from Lake Okeechobee south to Florida Bay.

- Tall sawgrass grows in the water of the Everglades. Low-lying islands are scattered throughout the sawgrass marsh.

Earth: The Water Planet

- The Everglades provide habitats for many rare organisms. The Florida panther is a large cat that lives there. Many kinds of large birds live in the Everglades.

- Water that once flowed into the Everglades is now used for farming and in homes. Canals and other structures have changed the way water flows through the Everglades. Some areas are drying up. Other areas are flooded.

- People have brought new plants and animals into the Everglades that had not lived there before. The new organisms compete for food and space with the organisms that have long made the Everglades their home.

Answer the following questions. Use your textbook and the ideas on page 17 and above.

4. A large wetland region in southern Florida is called the _____.

5. Circle the letter of each sentence that is true about the Everglades.
    a. The Everglades provide habitats for many rare organisms.
    b. Everglades National Park covers all of the Everglades.
    c. Water that once flowed into the Everglades is now used for farming and in homes.

6. Is the following sentence true or false? People have brought new plants and animals into the Everglades that had not lived there before. _____

Earth: The Water Planet

Importance of Wetlands (pages 32–33)

Key Concept: **Because of their sheltered waters and rich supply of nutrients, wetlands provide habitats for many living things.**

- Many organisms find habitats in wetlands. These include frogs, snails, turtles, and reed plants. Many insects and birds live in and around wetlands.

- Some organisms live in wetlands year round. Other organisms, such as geese, spend only part of a year in a wetland.

Answer the following question. Use your textbook and the ideas above.

7. Circle the letter of each sentence that is true about the importance of wetlands.

    a. Many organisms find habitats in wetlands.

    b. Wetlands have a rich supply of nutrients.

    c. No organisms live year round in wetlands.

Key Concept: **Wetlands act as natural water filters. They also help control floods by absorbing extra runoff from heavy rains.**

- Water moves slowly through a wetland. As the water slowly moves, waste materials settle to the ground. Other waste materials are taken in by plants. In this way, wetlands filter water and make the water cleaner.

- Wetlands act like giant sponges. They store water until it naturally evaporates or drains away. In this way, wetlands help control floods.

Answer the following question. Use your textbook and the ideas above.

8. Is the following sentence true or false? Wetlands act as natural water filters. _____

Earth: The Water Planet

Water Underground (pages 34–39)

How Water Moves Underground
(pages 34–35)

Key Concept: **Water underground trickles down between particles of soil and through cracks and spaces in layers of rock.**

- Rock and soil have spaces between their particles. The spaces between particles of rock or soil are called pores.

- When the pores of a material are connected, water can pass through easily. A material that water can pass easily through is called a **permeable** material. Sand and gravel are permeable materials.

- Some materials have few or no pores or cracks. A material that water cannot pass through easily is called an **impermeable** material. Clay and granite are impermeable materials.

- When water reaches an impermeable layer underground, the water is trapped. The water then fills up permeable rock or soil above. An area of permeable rock or soil that is totally filled with water is called the **saturated zone**. The top of the saturated zone is called the **water table**.

- Soil and rocks above the water table also contain water. The layer of rocks and soil above the water table is called the **unsaturated zone**.

Answer the following questions. Use your textbook and the ideas above.

1. Is the following sentence true or false? When the pores of a material are connected, water can pass through easily. _____

Earth: The Water Planet

2. Draw a line from each term to its meaning.

Term	Meaning
Term	**Meaning**
permeable material	**a.** the top of the saturated zone
	b. the layer of rocks and soil above the water table
impermeable material	**c.** a material that water can pass through easily
water table	**d.** an area of permeable rock or soil that is totally filled with water
saturated zone	
unsaturated zone	**e.** a material that water cannot pass through easily

3. The picture below shows the different materials that form layers underground. Circle the letter that points to the water table.

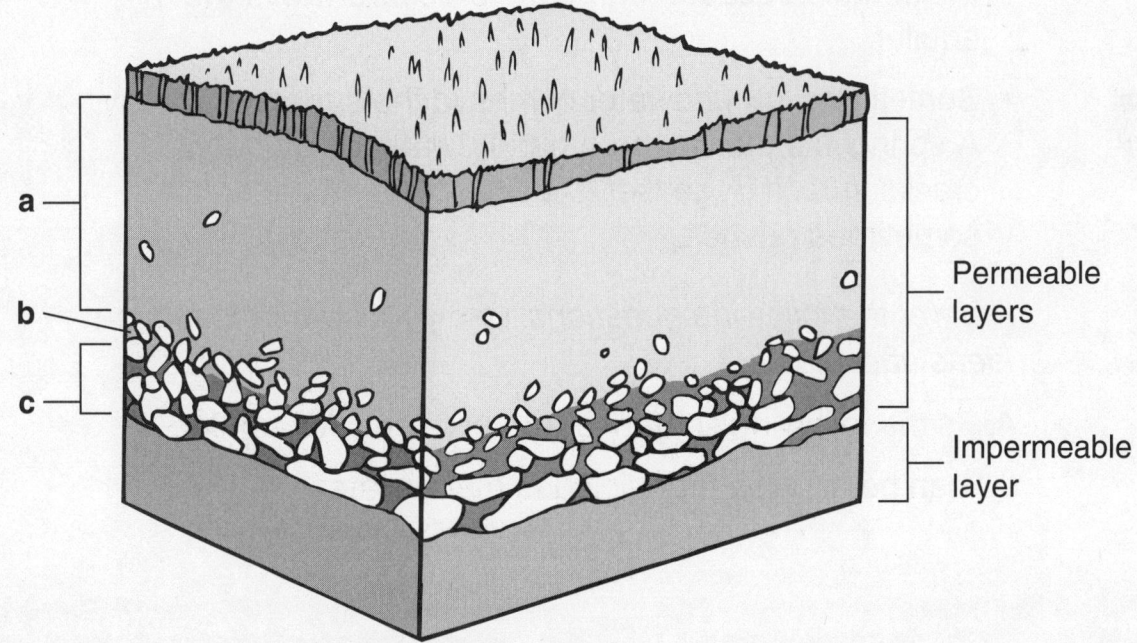

a

b

c

Permeable layers

Impermeable layer

Earth: The Water Planet

Bringing Up Groundwater (pages 36–39)

Key Concept: **People can obtain groundwater from an aquifer by drilling a well below the water table.**

- The water table in an area might be a few meters underground. In other areas it might be deep underground.

- An **aquifer** is an underground layer of rock or pieces of rock that holds water. An aquifer can be a small underground area, or it can be an area that includes many states.

- Since ancient times, people have brought groundwater to the surface by digging a well. A well must reach into the saturated zone.

- Most wells are dug with well-digging equipment. Pumps bring the groundwater to the surface.

- Sometimes, water underground is under great pressure. An **artesian** (ahr TEEZH un) **well** is where water rises to the surface because of natural pressure within the aquifer.

- Sometimes, groundwater comes to the surface naturally. A spring is a place where groundwater flows out of cracks in rock. A geyser is a hot spring where water sometimes gushes.

Answer the following questions. Use your textbook and the ideas above.

4. Is the following sentence true or false? An aquifer

   can be an area that includes many states. _____

Earth: The Water Planet

5. Read each word in the box. In each sentence below, fill in the correct word or words.

| artesian well | wetland | aquifer |

a. An underground layer of rock or pieces of rock that holds water is a(an) _____.

b. A well in which water rises to the surface because of natural pressure within the aquifer is a(an)

_____.

6. Circle the letter of each sentence that is true about bringing up groundwater.

a. Most wells are dug with well-digging equipment.

b. A spring is a place where groundwater flows out of cracks in rock.

c. For a well to work, the bottom of the well must reach into the unsaturated zone.

Freshwater Resources

Water Supply and Demand
(pages 48–55)

How People Use Water (pages 49–51)

Key Concept: People use water for household purposes, industry, transportation, agriculture, and recreation.

- People need water in homes for many uses.

- Many industries use water to cool hot machinery. Power plants and steel mills also use water for cooling.

- Since ancient times, people have used boats on water to carry people and products.

- Farmers need water to grow crops. **Irrigation** is when water is supplied to areas of land so crops can be grown.

- People use water to have fun, such as for boating and swimming.

Answer the following questions. Use your textbook and the ideas above.

1. The process of supplying water to areas of land so crops can be grown is called _____.

2. Circle the letter of each sentence that is true about how people use water.
    a. People use boats on water to carry people and products.
    b. People who farm have no special need for water.
    c. People need water in homes for many uses.

3. Complete the concept map about how people use water.

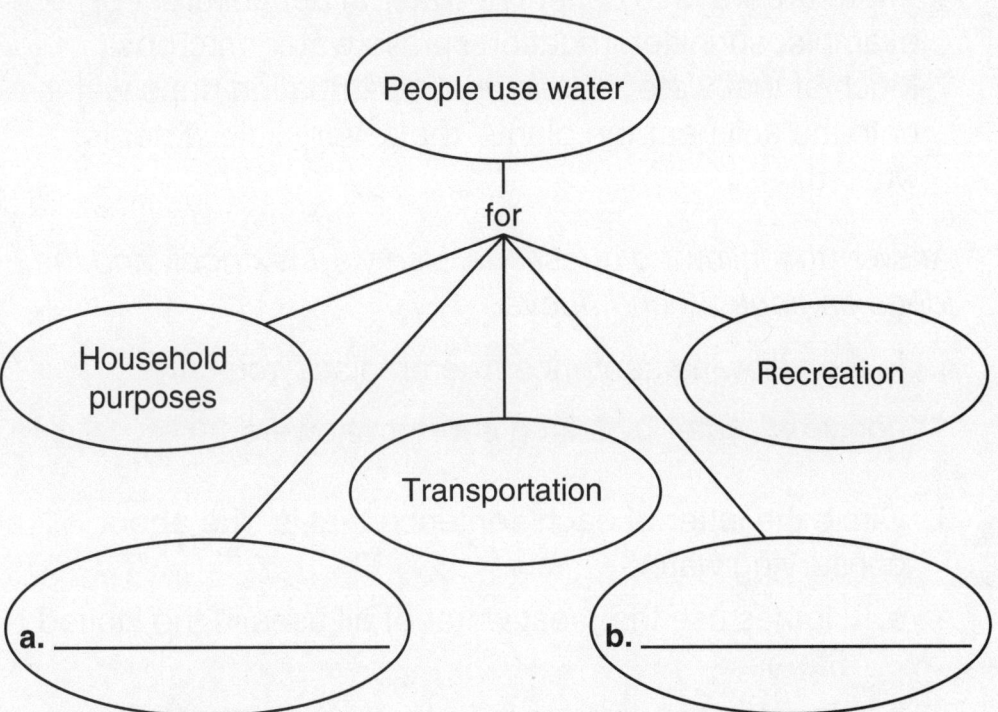

Conserving Water (pages 52–53)

***Key Concept:* Reducing water use, recycling water, and reusing water are three ways to conserve water.**

- People often use more water than they really need. You can conserve water at home by doing simple things, such as taking shorter showers.

- New water-saving methods help industries save money and obey environmental laws.

- Some industries conserve water by building cooling pools. That way, the water in the pool can be used over and over.

- Agriculture, or farming, uses the most water of all uses in the United States.

- There are ways to conserve water in agriculture. For example, sprinkler irrigation sprays water on crops. Much of that water is wasted. Drip irrigation drips water onto the soil near the plants' roots. Very little water is wasted.

Answer the following questions. Use your textbook and the ideas on page 25 and above.

4. Is the following sentence true or false? You can

   conserve water by taking shorter showers. _____

5. Circle the letter of each sentence that is true about conserving water.

   a. Homes use the most water of all uses in the United States.

   b. People often use more water than they really need.

   c. New water-saving methods help industries save money.

6. Is the following sentence true or false? Drip irrigation wastes more water than sprinkler irrigation.

   _____

Fresh Water for the Future (pages 54–55)

Key Concept: **Two possible methods of obtaining fresh water for the future are desalination and melting icebergs.**

- **Desalination** is when the salt is removed from salt water to make fresh water. There are several ways to desalinate water. All ways are very expensive.

Freshwater Resources

- One method of desalination is called distillation. First the water is boiled. The water vapor that forms is then cooled to produce liquid water.

- Icebergs are made up of frozen fresh water. Melting an iceberg could provide millions of liters of fresh water.

Answer the following questions. Use your textbook and the ideas on page 26 and above.

7. A process that removes salt from salt water to make

fresh water is called _____.

8. Circle the letter of each sentence that is true about obtaining fresh water for the future.

    a. One possible method of obtaining fresh water is by melting icebergs.

    b. All methods of desalination do not cost very much money.

    c. A method of desalination called distillation involves boiling water.

Name _____ Date _____ Class _____

Freshwater Resources

Water to Drink (pages 57–63)

Water Quality (pages 58–59)

Key Concept: **Certain substances, such as iron, can affect the taste or color of water but are harmless unless present at very high levels. Other substances, such as certain chemicals and microorganisms, can be harmful to your health.**

- **Water quality** is a measure of the substances in water other than the water molecules.

- The government sets concentration limits for some substances. A **concentration** is how much there is of one substance in a certain volume of another substance. Concentrations are often measured in parts per million (ppm).

- The pH of water also affects its quality. The **pH** of water is a measure of how acidic or basic the water is.

- **Hardness** is a measure of how much of two minerals there is in a sample of water. The two minerals are calcium and magnesium. Hard water contains high levels of calcium and magnesium.

Answer the following questions. Use your textbook and the ideas above.

1. Is the following sentence true or false? Certain substances in water are harmless unless they are present at very high levels. _____

2. Concentrations are often measured in parts per _____.

3. Complete the table of terms related to water quality.

Terms Related to Water Quality	
Term	**Meaning**
a. _____	how much there is of one substance in a certain volume of another substance
b. _____	a measure of how acidic or basic the water is
c. _____	a measure of how much calcium and magnesium there is in a sample of water

Treating Drinking Water (pages 60–62)

***Key Concept:* Water from both public and private supplies often needs some treatment to ensure that it is clean and safe to drink.**

- Water treatment is a way to make water safe to drink. Water treatment often takes place in a water treatment plant.

- The first step of drinking-water treatment is usually filtration. **Filtration** is when water is passed through a series of screens. The screens do not allow large objects to pass through.

- The second step is coagulation. **Coagulation** is when a chemical is added to water to make particles stick together. The chemical causes sticky globs to form. These globs are then filtered out of the water.

Freshwater Resources

- The next step is to add chlorine to the water. Chlorine is a chemical that kills organisms that cause disease.

- The next step is to force air through the water. This reduces bad odors and tastes.

Answer the following questions. Use your textbook and the ideas on page 29 and above.

4. Is the following sentence true or false? Water treatment is a way to make water clean and safe to drink.

_____

5. The picture below shows drinking-water treatment. Draw arrows to show the direction that water moves through a water treatment plant.

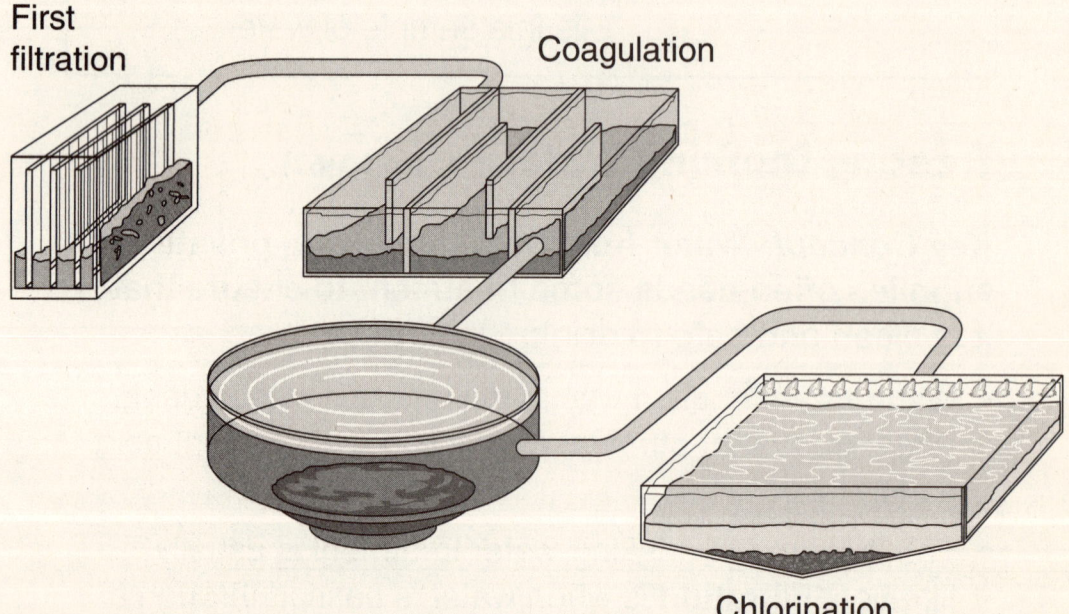

First filtration

Coagulation

Chlorination

Freshwater Resources

6. Draw a line from each term to its meaning.

Term	Meaning
filtration	**a.** the process of particles sticking together
coagulation	**b.** the process of passing water through a series of screens

Treating Wastewater (pages 62–63)

Key Concept: **Two ways that communities deal with sewage are wastewater treatment plants and septic systems.**

- Wastewater and the different kinds of waste in it are called **sewage**.

- In most communities, household wastewater flows into a system of pipes called sanitary sewers. The sanitary sewers carry the wastewater to a wastewater treatment plant.

- Some people treat their sewage using a septic system. A septic system has an underground tank. Bacteria in the tank break down materials in the water as the water passes through the tank.

Answer the following questions. Use your textbook and the ideas above.

7. Wastewater and the different kinds of waste in it are called _____.

8. Is the following sentence true or false? Most communities treat sewage in a wastewater treatment plant. _____

Freshwater Resources

Freshwater Pollution (pages 68–77)

What Is Pollution? (pages 69–70)

Key Concept: Sources of pollution are classified, in part, by how they enter a body of water.

- **Water pollution** is adding any substance to water that has a bad effect on the water or the living things in the water. The substances that cause water pollution are called **pollutants**.

- A **point source** is a specific source of pollution that can be identified. For example, a pipe pouring polluted water into a river is a point source.

- A widely spread source of pollution is called a **nonpoint source**. For example, pollutants in runoff from a farm field make up a nonpoint source.

- Some pollutants can build up in the bodies of living things. Pesticides are an example. **Pesticides** are chemicals used to kill insects and other pests. Pesticides that pollute water can harm living things.

Answer the following questions. Use your textbook and the ideas above.

1. Circle the letter of each sentence that is true about pollution.
   a. Sources of pollution are classified by how they enter a body of water.
   b. Pesticides that pollute water can harm living things.
   c. A pipe pouring bad water into a river is a nonpoint source.

2. Draw a line from each term to its meaning.

Term	Meaning
water pollution	**a.** a widely spread source of pollution
pollutant	**b.** a specific source of pollution that can be identified
point source	**c.** adding any substance to water that has a bad effect on the water or the living things in the water
nonpoint source	
pesticide	**d.** a chemical used to kill insects and other pests
	e. a substance that causes water pollution

Human Wastes (page 71)

Key Concept: **Human wastes are one of the three major sources of water pollution.**

• Dumping human wastes into drinking water can cause disease.

• Wastewater is usually treated before it goes into the environment. Wastewater treatment kills most bacteria. But some germs survive and get into the drinking-water supply.

• Septic tanks are commonly used outside of cities. People should not put septic tanks too close to streams or wells.

• Animal wastes from cattle, pigs, and chickens can also pollute water in farm areas. Animal wastes can run off fields into streams and rivers.

Freshwater Resources

Answer the following questions. Use your textbook and the ideas on page 33.

3. Circle the letter of each sentence that is true about pollution caused by human wastes.

   a. People should not put septic tanks too near a well.

   b. Dumping human wastes into drinking water can cause disease.

   c. Wastewater treatment is not able to kill any types of bacteria.

4. Is the following sentence true or false? Animal wastes can pollute water in farm areas. _____

Industrial Wastes (pages 72–73)

Key Concept: **Industrial wastes are a second major source of water pollution.**

- Water pollution from factories and mines is a serious problem. Chemicals, smoke, and heated water are three types of pollutants produced by factories and mines.

- Some factories let chemicals go into nearby rivers and lakes. This is against the law. Some industries store chemicals in barrels underground. These barrels can leak. The chemicals can pollute the soil and groundwater.

- Many power plants and factories burn coal or oil. Cars and trucks burn gasoline. Burning coal, oil, and gasoline puts chemicals in the air that cause acid rain. **Acid rain** has more acid than normal rain. Acid rain falls on lakes and ponds. Then fish and other living things cannot survive.

- Heated water released by factories can harm living things in nearby rivers or ponds.

Name _____ Date _____ Class _____

Freshwater Resources

Answer the following questions. Use your textbook and the ideas on page 34.

5. Complete the concept map about types of pollutants produced by factories and mines.

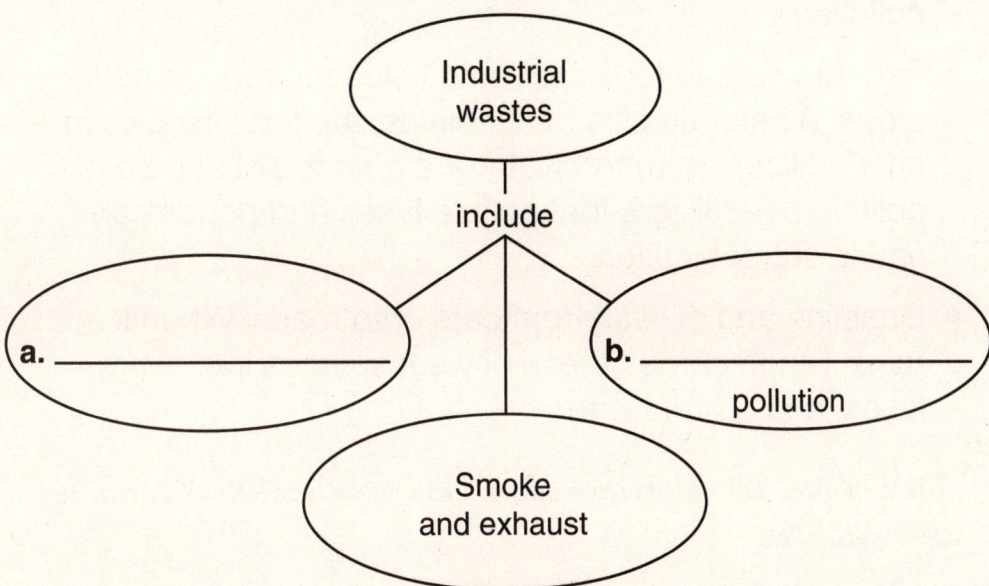

6. Rain that has more acid than normal rain is called

_____.

7. Is the following sentence true or false? Burning coal, oil, and gasoline puts chemicals in the air that cause

acid rain. _____

Freshwater Resources

Chemical Runoff (page 74)

Key Concept: **Chemical wastes are a third major source of water pollution.**

- Runoff from farm fields and roads causes water pollution.

- Farmers spread fertilizers onto fields to produce better crops. When rain falls on the fields, the fertilizers wash off. Fertilizers in runoff water are a nonpoint source of pollution. Fertilizers that pollute lakes and ponds can cause eutrophication.

- Gasoline and oil leak from cars onto roads. When it rains, runoff carries these oily substances into rivers, lakes, and groundwater.

Answer the following question. Use your textbook and the ideas above.

8. Circle the letter of each sentence that is true about chemical runoff.

　　a. When it rains, runoff carries oily substances from roads into rivers.

　　b. Runoff from farm fields and roads causes water pollution.

　　c. Fertilizers in runoff are a nonpoint source of pollution.

Water Pollution Solutions (pages 75–77)

Key Concept: **Solving pollution problems involves cleaning up existing problems as well as preventing new ones.**

- Living things in lakes, streams, and wetlands help reduce pollution. These living things filter out and break down waste materials.

Freshwater Resources

- Plant roots filter large particles from water. Some bacteria break down harmful chemicals in rivers and lakes.

- People have built wetlands near coal mines to treat mining runoff before it returns to the environment.

- Many industries recycle water. Recycling reduces water pollution.

- Some farmers collect runoff from fields and barnyards to use for watering crops. Some farmers plant grasses that filter out pollutants before runoff reaches rivers and ponds.

- You can prevent water pollution by throwing away chemicals and other harmful substances in safe ways.

Answer the following questions. Use your textbook and the ideas on page 36 and above.

9. Is the following sentence true or false? Living things in lakes, streams, and wetlands help reduce pollution by filtering out and breaking down waste materials.

_____

10. Circle the letter of each sentence that is true about water pollution solutions.

    a. Some farmers collect runoff from fields and barnyards to use for watering crops.

    b. Recycling water in industry does not reduce water pollution.

    c. You can prevent water pollution throwing away harmful substances in safe ways.

Freshwater Resources

Droughts and Floods (pages 78-83)

Droughts (pages 78-79)

Key Concept: **Droughts are usually caused by dry weather systems that remain in one place for weeks or months at a time.**

- A **drought** (drowt) is a long period of very little rainfall. A drought lowers the supply of both groundwater and surface water.

- Long droughts can badly hurt a region. Droughts can cause crops to fail. Streams and ponds dry up. Both people and animals suffer.

- When droughts occur, people can conserve water by not washing cars or watering lawns. Farmers can grow plants that do not need a lot of water.

Answer the following questions. Use your textbook and the ideas above.

1. A long period of very little rainfall is a(an)

   _____.

2. Is the following sentence true or false? Droughts are usually caused by dry weather systems. _____

Floods (pages 80-81)

Key Concept: **All floods occur when the volume of water in a river increases so much that the river overflows its channel.**

- As rain and melting snow add water to a river, the river gains in speed and strength. A flooding river can uproot trees and pull large rocks from the ground. Powerful flood waters can even wash away bridges and buildings.

Freshwater Resources

• Flash floods are the most dangerous weather-related events in the United States. A **flash flood** is a sudden, violent flood that occurs within a few minutes or a few hours after a storm begins.

• Most flash floods are caused by large amounts of rain. A hurricane or a thunderstorm can cause a flash flood. A flash flood can also be caused by a dam breaking.

Answer the following questions. Use your textbook and the ideas on page 38 and above.

3. A sudden, violent flood that occurs within a few minutes or a few hours after a storm begins is a(an)

_____.

4. Complete the concept map about flash floods.

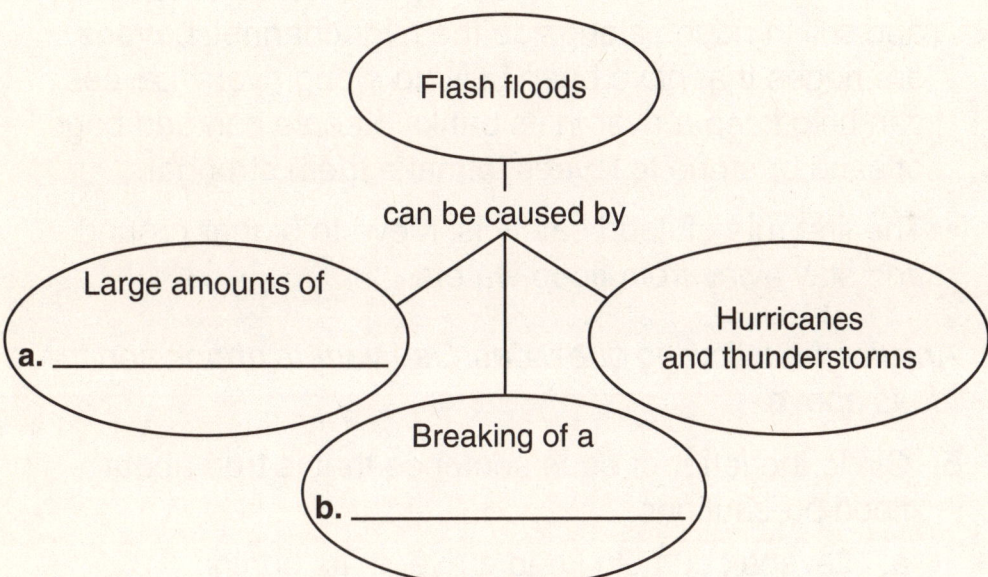

Freshwater Resources

Flood Precautions (pages 82–83)

Key Concept: **Advance warnings help reduce flood damage and loss of life. Building dams is one method of flood control.**

- Radar and satellites are used to predict when a river might flood. When people hear that a river might flood, they can prepare. People might even have to leave an area that will flood.

- A dam is a barrier across a river. A dam can send water into other channels or create a lake. Engineers can open gates in a dam to release water in dry seasons. Dams work well to control small floods. During large floods, though, flood waters can wash over the top of a dam or break through a dam.

- When a river overflows its banks, the water leaves rock and soil in ridges alongside the river channel. **Levees** are ridges that have been built up along rivers. Levees can help keep a river in its banks. People can add bags of sand or stone to levees to make them stronger.

- The first rule of flood safety is: Move to higher ground and stay away from flood waters.

Answer the following questions. Use your textbook and the ideas above.

5. Circle the letter of each sentence that is true about flood precautions.

    a. Levees can help keep a river in its banks.

    b. Advance warnings help reduce flood damage.

    c. Dams work well to control large floods.

6. A ridge that has been built up naturally along a river is a(an) _____.

Freshwater Resources

Water Power (pages 84–87)

Energy and Moving Water (page 85)

Key Concept: **Hydroelectric power plants capture the kinetic energy of moving water and change it into electrical energy.**

- **Kinetic energy** is the form of energy that an object has when it is moving. **Potential energy** is energy that is stored and waiting to be used. Energy can change from one form to another.

- **Hydroelectric power** is electricity produced by the kinetic energy of water moving over a waterfall or through a dam. Hydroelectric power is also called "hydropower."

- To make hydropower, engineers build a dam across a river. Water backs up behind the dam. The water behind the dam has potential energy. The water's potential energy is changed to kinetic energy when the water is released.

Answer the following questions. Use your textbook and the ideas above.

1. Read each word in the box. In each sentence below, fill in the correct words.

potential energy	electrical energy
kinetic energy	

   a. The form of energy that an object has when it is moving is called _____.

   b. Energy that is stored and waiting to be used is called _____.

Freshwater Resources

2. Electricity produced by the kinetic energy of water moving over a waterfall or through a dam is called

_____.

3. The picture below shows a dam built across a river in order to produce hydroelectric power. Make an X on the place where water has potential energy.

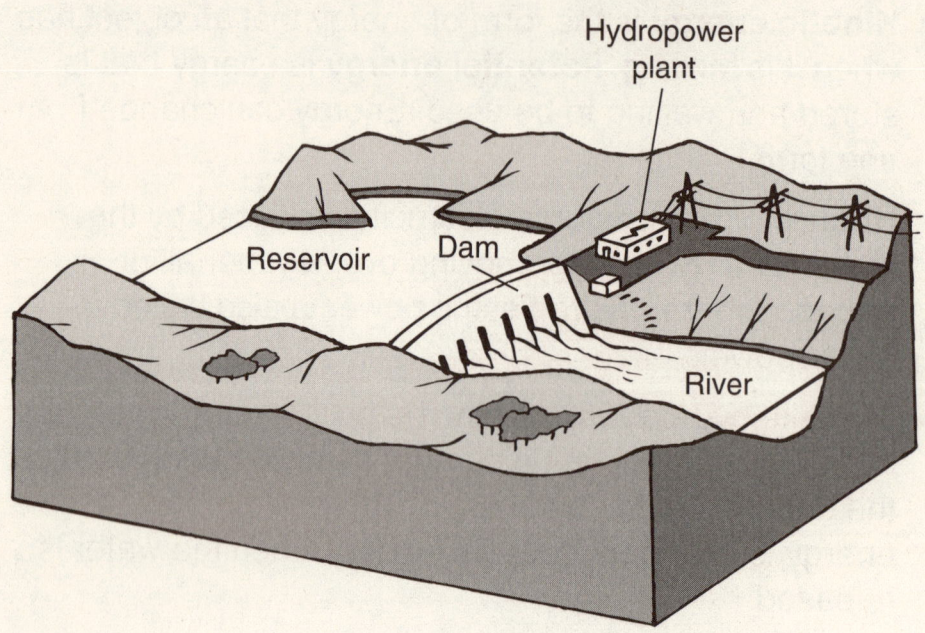

Hydroelectric Power Plants (pages 86–87)

Key Concept: **Hydroelectric power is clean, safe, and efficient. Building a dam is expensive, but the water is free and is naturally renewed by the water cycle.**

• A hydroelectric power plant changes the kinetic energy of moving water into electrical energy. The electrical energy lights homes and runs computers.

• An advantage of hydroelectric power is that hydroelectric plants do not cause air pollution.

Freshwater Resources

Answer the following question. Use your textbook and the ideas on page 42.

4. Circle the letter of each sentence that is true about the advantages of hydroelectric power.

    a. Building a dam is cheap to do.

    b. Hydroelectric plants do not cause air pollution.

    c. Hydroelectric power is efficient.

Key Concept: Flooding the land behind a dam can destroy wildlife habitats as well as farms and towns. In addition, the dam forms a barrier across the river.

- Dams affect all living things in the areas around them. Some organisms cannot survive the change from a fast-flowing river to a lake environment.

- Dams can prevent some fish from swimming to parts of a river where they usually lay eggs and hatch young.

Answer the following question. Use your textbook and the ideas above.

5. Circle the letter of each sentence that is true about the disadvantages of hydroelectric power.

    a. Dams can prevent some fish from swimming to parts of a river where they usually lay eggs.

    b. Flooding the land behind a dam can destroy wildlife habitats.

    c. Flooding the land behind a dam protects all wildlife habitats.

Ocean Motions

Wave Action (pages 94–101)

What Is a Wave? (pages 95–96)

Key Concept: **Most waves form when winds blowing across the water's surface transmit their energy to the water.**

- A water **wave** is the movement of energy through a body of water.

- The size of a wave depends on two factors:
  1. the strength of the wind
  2. the length of time the wind blows

- Waves do not actually carry water forward. The energy of a wave moves toward a shore, but the water itself stays in place. As a wave passes a place, water particles move in a circle. The particles move forward and down with the energy of the wave and then back to their original positions.

- The highest part of a wave is called the crest. A **wavelength** is the distance from one crest to the next crest.

- Waves are also measured by their frequency. **Frequency** is the number of waves that pass a point in a certain amount of time.

- The lowest part of a wave is called the trough. **Wave height** is the up-and-down distance from a crest to a trough.

Answer the following questions. Use your textbook and the ideas above.

1. Is the following sentence true or false? Waves do not actually carry water forward. _____

Ocean Motions

2. Read each word in the box. In each sentence below, fill in the correct word or words.

wave	wavelength	frequency
wave height	crest	

a. The distance from one crest to the next crest is a

_____.

b. A water _____ is the movement of energy through a body of water.

c. The up-and-down distance from a crest to a

trough is called the _____.

d. The number of waves that pass a point in a certain

amount of time is the _____ of the waves.

3. The picture below shows a water wave. Draw a line that shows the wavelength of this wave.

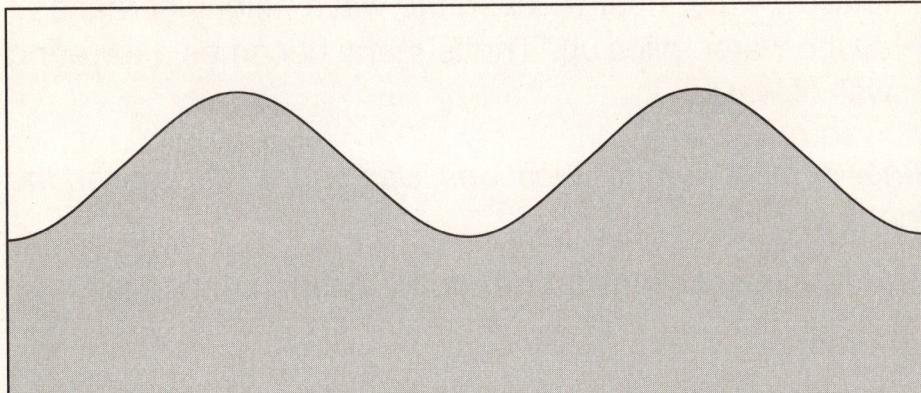

Ocean Motions

Ocean Motions

How Waves Change Near Shore (pages 97–98)

Key Concept: **Near shore, wave height increases and wavelength decreases.**

- The white-capped waves that crash onto an ocean shore are often called "breakers." As a wave comes near to shore, the wave slows down. As it slows down, its shape changes. When a wave reaches a certain height, the crest of the wave falls. The wave "breaks" onto the shore.

- A breaker moves up the beach, but gravity stops it. The water then flows back out to sea. This rush of water out to sea is called an undertow. A strong undertow can be dangerous to swimmers.

- A **tsunami** is a wave that forms far below the ocean surface. Earthquakes under the ocean floor cause tsunamis. When a tsunami reaches a coast, it can destroy buildings and bridges.

- A tsunami in deep water may have a long wavelength but a small wave height. When the tsunami reaches shallow water near a coast, the wave height increases as the water "piles up." The tsunami becomes a towering wall of water.

Answer the following questions. Use your textbook and the ideas above.

4. A wave that forms far below the ocean surface is

 a(an) _____.

5. Is the following sentence true or false? The rush of water flowing back out to sea is called an undertow.

 _____

Ocean Motions

6. Circle the letter of each sentence that is true about how waves change near shore.

   a. When the tsunami reaches shallow water near a coast, the wave height increases.

   b. As waves come near a shore, the waves slow down.

   c. Near shore, wave height decreases and wave length increases.

How Waves Affect the Shore (page 99)

Key Concept: **As waves come into shore, water washes up the beach at an angle, carrying sand grains. The water and sand then run straight back down the beach.**

- Winds far out at sea affect the direction of waves. As a result, waves usually come toward shore at an angle.

- Water flows up a beach at an angle, but the water flows straight back out to sea—not at the angle it flowed in. The result is the movement of sand along the beach. **Longshore drift** is the movement of sand along a beach.

- As waves slow down, they drop the sand they are carrying. The sand forms a long underwater ridge called a sandbar.

- As a sandbar grows, it can trap the water flowing along the shore. In some places, water rushing back out to sea breaks through the sandbar, creating a narrow opening. A **rip current** is a rush of water that flows rapidly back to sea through a narrow opening.

Ocean Motions

Answer the following questions. Use your textbook and the ideas on page 47.

7. Complete the table of terms related to how waves affect a shore.

Terms Related to How Waves Affect a Shore	
Term	**Meaning**
a. _____ _____	the movement of sand along a beach
b. _____	a long underwater ridge of sand
c. _____ _____	a rush of water that flows rapidly back to sea through a narrow opening in a sandbar

8. Circle the letter of what causes longshore drift.

    a. Water flows up a beach at an angle, but the water flows straight back out to sea.

    b. In some places, water rushing back out to sea breaks through the sandbar.

    c. Water flows straight up a beach, but the water flows at an angle back out to sea.

9. Is the following sentence true or false? As waves slow down, they drop the sand they are carrying.

    _____

Waves and Beach Erosion (pages 100–101)

Key Concept: **Waves shape a beach by eroding the shore in some places and building it up in others.**

- The area between the land and an ocean is always changing. Over time, waves break rocks into pebbles and grains of sand. Longshore drift moves sand along a coast. This breaking up of rock and carrying it away is called erosion.

- Long sand deposits called barrier beaches form along a shore. Barrier beaches are separated from the mainland by shallow water. Barrier beaches protect shorelines from the force of waves. Waves break against the barrier beaches instead of against the shore.

- Erosion can wear away beaches. This causes problems for homes and other buildings near beaches. One way to reduce beach erosion is by building groins. A **groin** is a wall of rocks or concrete that is built straight out from a beach. Sand carried by water piles up against the groins instead of moving along a shore.

Answer the following questions. Use your textbook and the ideas above.

10. A wall of rocks or concrete that is built straight out

   from a beach is a(an) _____.

11. Circle the letter of each sentence that is true about waves and beach erosion.

   a. The process of breaking up rock and carrying it away is called longshore drift.

   b. Barrier beaches protect shorelines from the force of waves.

   c. One way to reduce beach erosion is by building groins.

Ocean Motions

Tides (pages 102–107)

What Causes Tides? (pages 103–106)

Key Concept: **Tides are caused by the interaction of Earth, the moon, and the sun.**

- **Tides** are the daily rise and fall of Earth's waters on its coastlines.

- As a tide comes in, the level of water rises. High tide is when the water is highest. Then the tide flows out, flowing back toward the sea. Low tide is when the water reaches its lowest point.

- Gravity causes tides. Gravity is the force an object has that pulls other objects toward it.

- The moon's gravity pulls on Earth's waters. The moon's gravity creates a bulge of water on the side of Earth closest to the moon. The water on the other side of Earth forms a second bulge. These are called tidal bulges. In places where there are tidal bulges, high tide occurs.

- In many places, there are two high tides and two low tides each day. In other places, one set of tides is so small that it seems like there is only one high tide and one low tide per day.

Answer the following questions. Use your textbook and the ideas above.

1. Circle the letter of each sentence that is true about tides.

    a. High tide is when the water is highest.

    b. In many places, there are two high tides a day.

    c. In places where there are tidal bulges, low tide occurs.

Ocean Motions

2. The daily rise and fall of Earth's waters on its coastlines are called _____.

3. Is the following sentence true or false? Gravity causes tides. _____

Key Concept: **Changes in the positions of Earth, the moon, and the sun affect the heights of the tides during a month.**

- The sun's gravity also affects Earth's tides. The sun pulls the water on Earth's surface toward it.

- When the sun and the moon are lined up, their gravities combine to produce a spring tide. A **spring tide** is a tide with the greatest difference between high tide and low tide.

- When the sun and the moon are at right angles to each other, the sun's gravity pulls some water away from tidal bulges. The result is a neap tide. A **neap tide** is a tide with the least difference between high tide and low tide.

Answer the following questions. Use your textbook and the ideas above.

4. Complete the table about kinds of tides.

Kinds of Tides	
Kind of Tide	**Description**
a. _____ _____	a tide with the greatest difference between high tide and low tide
b. _____ _____	a tide with the least difference between high tide and low tide

5. The picture below shows the Earth, moon, and sun. Circle the letter of the kind of tide that occurs when the Earth, moon, and sun are in line like this.

    a. low tide

    b. spring tide

    c. neap tide

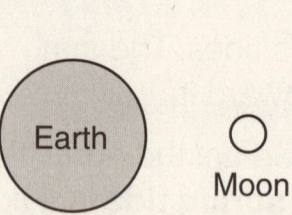 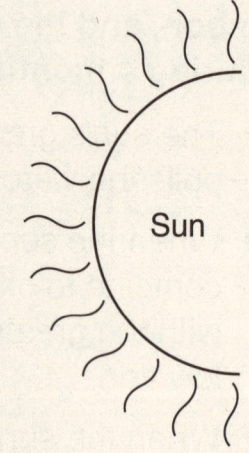

Energy From Tides (pages 106–107)

Key Concept: **The movement of huge amounts of water between high and low tide is a source of potential energy—energy that is stored and can be used.**

- A lot of water moves between high and low tides. In some places, tidal power plants use the energy of tides to produce electricity.

- The energy of tides is used only in places where there is a big difference between high tide and low tide. There are very few places in the world with such a big difference.

Answer the following question. Use your textbook and the ideas above.

6. In some places, tidal power plants use the energy of tides to produce _____.

Ocean Water Chemistry (pages 108–113)

The Salty Ocean (pages 109–110)

Key Concept: On average, one kilogram of ocean water contains about 35 grams of salts—that is, 35 parts per thousand.

- If you boiled a kilogram of ocean water in a pot until all the water was gone, there would be about 35 grams of salt left in the pot.

- **Salinity** is the total amount of dissolved salts in a sample of water.

- Sodium chloride—table salt—makes up most of the salts in ocean water. There are also other kinds of salts in ocean water.

- The salinity of ocean water is not always the same. In most parts of the ocean, salinity is between 34 and 37 parts per thousand. Near the mouths of large rivers, salinity is lower because rivers bring fresh water.

- Salinity affects the properties of water. Ocean water freezes at a lower temperature than fresh water. Also, ocean water is denser than fresh water. As a result, you can float more easily in ocean water than in fresh water.

Answer the following questions. Use your textbook and the ideas above.

1. The total amount of dissolved salts in a sample of

   water is _____.

2. Most of the salt in salt water is sodium chloride, or

   _____.

Ocean Motions

3. The circle graph below shows the makeup of ocean water. Circle the letter of what makes up 35 parts per thousand.

   a. water molecules

   b. carbon dioxide and other gases

   c. sodium chloride and other salts

Makeup of Ocean Water

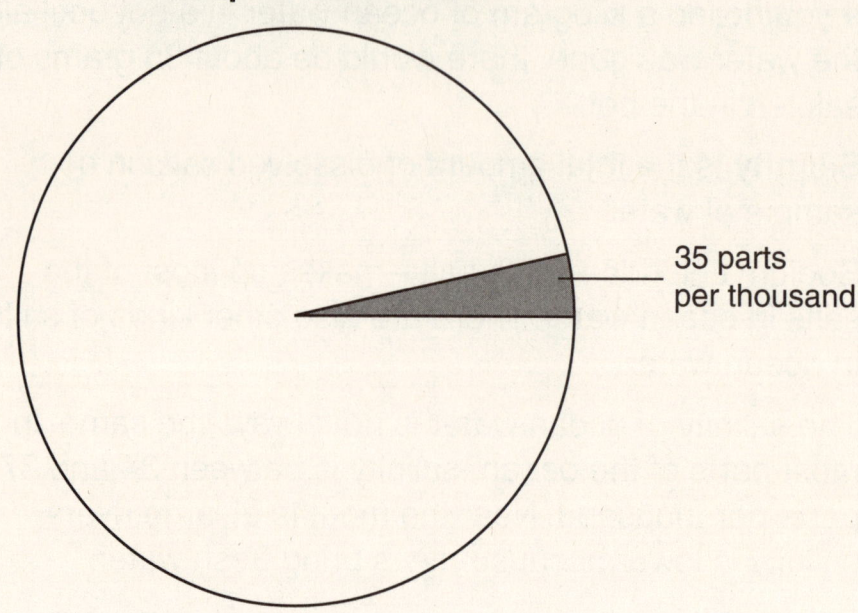

35 parts per thousand

4. Is the following sentence true or false? Near the mouths of large rivers, salinity is higher.

_____

Other Ocean Properties (page 111)

Key Concept: **Like temperatures on land, temperatures at the surface of the ocean vary with location and the seasons. Gases in ocean water vary as well.**

• The ocean absorbs energy from the sun. Near the equator, the temperature at the surface of the ocean is about 25°C—about room temperature. The temperature drops as you go away from the equator.

Ocean Motions

- The deeper you go in the ocean, the colder and denser the water is. Cold water is denser than warm water.

- Ocean organisms use gases in ocean water. Two gases that ocean organisms use are carbon dioxide and oxygen. Algae, for example, need carbon dioxide to carry out photosynthesis. Ocean animals need oxygen.

- There is much more carbon dioxide in the ocean than in the air. There is much less oxygen in the ocean than in the air. Surface water has more oxygen in it than deeper water has.

Answer the following questions. Use your textbook and the ideas on page 54 and above.

5. Circle the letter of each sentence that is true about ocean properties.

   a. The deeper you go in the ocean, the denser the water is.

   b. The temperature of ocean water drops as you go away from the equator.

   c. Ocean water contains oxygen but not carbon dioxide.

6. Is the following sentence true or false? Deep water has more oxygen in it than surface water. _____

Changes With Depth (page 113)

Key Concept: **As you descend through the ocean, the water temperature decreases. Pressure increases continuously with depth in the ocean.**

- If you could drop from the ocean's surface to the ocean floor, you would pass through a section of the ocean known as the water column. Conditions change as you go from the top of the water column to the bottom.

Ocean Motions

- There are three temperature zones in the water column. The surface zone is warmest. The transition zone begins at about 1 kilometer down. Temperatures drop quickly in the transition zone. Below the transition zone is the deep zone, where the water is very cold.

- Water pressure is the force of the weight of water. Because of high pressure in the deep ocean, divers can go down safely to only about 40 meters.

Answer the following questions. Use your textbook and the ideas on page 55 and above.

7. Is the following sentence true or false? Pressure

   increases the deeper you go in the ocean. _____

8. Complete the table about the three temperature zones in the ocean water column.

Temperature Zones in the Ocean Water Column	
Zone	**Description**
a. _____ zone	the warmest zone, which goes down to 100–500 meters
Transition zone	the zone that goes from the surface zone down to about 1 kilometer
b. _____ zone	the bottom zone, where temperatures average 3.5°C

Currents and Climate (pages 116–121)

Surface Currents (pages 117–119)

Key Concept: **Surface currents, which affect water to a depth of several hundred meters, are driven mainly by winds.**

- A **current** is a large stream of moving water that flows through the oceans. Unlike waves, currents carry water from place to place.

- Surface currents move in circular patterns in the oceans. Most currents flow east or west, and then turn back to complete the circle.

- Earth rotates on its axis. The effect that Earth's rotation has on the direction of winds and currents is called the **Coriolis** (kawr ee OH lis) **effect**. The Coriolis effect causes ocean currents to move in circular patterns.

- The largest and most powerful surface current in the North Atlantic Ocean is called the Gulf Stream. It moves northward along the east coast of the United States.

Answer the following questions. Use your textbook and the ideas above.

1. A large stream of moving water that flows through the oceans is a(an) _____.

2. Circle the letter of each sentence that is true about surface currents.
   a. The Gulf Stream moves northward along the east coast of the United States.
   b. Surface currents are driven mainly by differences in density.
   c. Surface currents move in circular patterns in the oceans.

Ocean Motions

3. The effect that Earth's rotation has on the direction of winds and ocean currents is called the

_____ effect.

Key Concept: **A surface current warms or cools the air above it, influencing the climate of the land near the coast.**

- **Climate** is the pattern of temperature and precipitation that is usual in an area over a long time.

- Currents affect climate by moving cold and warm water around the world. Some currents carry warm water from the equator to the poles. Other currents carry cold water from the poles to the equator. Warm water warms the air above it. Cold water cools the air above.

- Sometimes, changes in wind patterns and currents occur. Such changes can have big effects on oceans and the land nearby.

- One example of a change in wind patterns and currents is El Niño. **El Niño** is an uncommon climate event that happens every two to seven years in the Pacific Ocean. During an El Niño, warm water moves toward the South American coast. This climate event can affect the climate of places far away.

Answer the following questions. Use your textbook and the ideas above.

4. Draw a line from each term to its meaning.

Term	Meaning
climate	**a.** uncommon climate event that happens every two to seven years in the Pacific Ocean
El Niño	
	b. the pattern of temperature and precipitation that is usual in an area over a long time

5. Is the following sentence true or false? Warm water cools the air above it. _____

Deep Currents (page 120)

Key Concept: **Deep currents are caused by differences in the density of ocean water. Deep currents move and mix water around the world. They carry cold water from the poles toward the equator.**

- The density of water depends on the water's temperature and salinity. When warm water flows toward the poles, the water gets cooler. Some of the water freezes and becomes ice. When water freezes, it leaves its salts behind. That causes the salinity of the remaining water to be higher.

- As the water gets colder and its salinity gets higher, the water becomes denser. Dense water sinks.

- The cold water deep in the ocean flows along the ocean floor toward the equator as a deep current.

- Deep currents flow very slowly.

Answer the following questions. Use your textbook and the ideas above.

6. Cold water that flows along the ocean floor toward the equator is a(an) _____.

7. Circle the letter of each sentence that is true about deep currents.
  a. Deep currents carry cold water from the poles toward the equator.
  b. Deep currents are caused by differences in the density of ocean water.
  c. Deep currents flow very quickly.

Ocean Motions

Upwelling (pages 120–121)

Key Concept: **Upwelling brings up tiny ocean organisms, minerals, and other nutrients from the deeper layers of the water. Without this motion, the surface waters of the open ocean would be very scarce in nutrients.**

- Sometimes, winds cause surface waters to mix with deep ocean waters. Winds blow away the warm surface water. Cold water from the deep ocean rises to replace the surface water.

- When cold water moves upward from the deep ocean, it is called **upwelling**.

- Places where upwelling occurs usually have many fish. This is because the rising water brings nutrients up from the deep ocean.

Answer the following question. Use your textbook and the ideas above.

8. The picture below shows the ocean near the coast of a continent. The arrows show wind, the movement of warm surface water, and upwelling from the deep ocean. Circle the arrows that show upwelling.

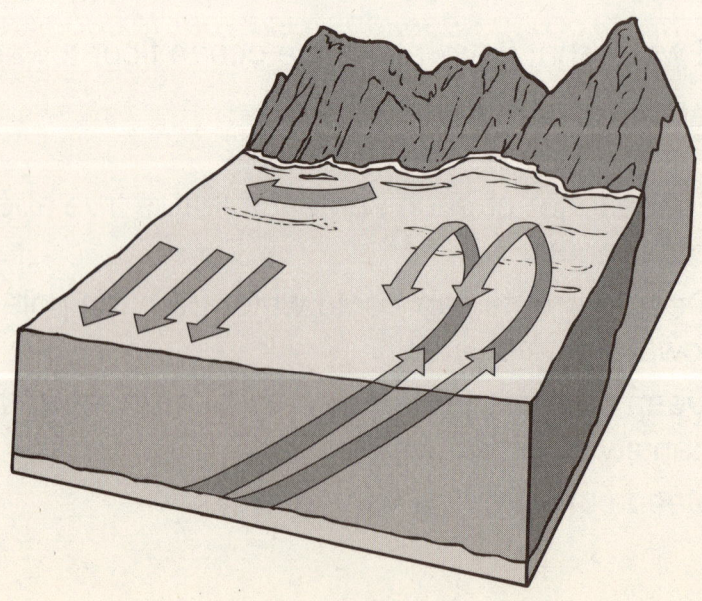

Exploring the Ocean (pages 130–139)

Learning About the Ocean (pages 131–133)

Key Concept: **People have studied the ocean since ancient times, because the ocean provides food and serves as a route for trade and travel. Modern scientists have studied the characteristics of the ocean's waters and the ocean floor.**

- People have been using the sea for trade for thousands of years.

- As trade increased in modern times, people needed good maps of the oceans and the lands nearby. In the 1700s and 1800s, most of Earth's coastlines had been mapped.

- Studying the ocean floor is difficult because the ocean is so deep. The deep ocean is dark, and the water is very cold. The pressure is very high in the deep ocean.

- It got easier to map the ocean floor when sonar was invented. Sonar stands for **so**und **na**vigation and **r**anging. **Sonar** is a system that uses sound waves to find the distance to an object.

Answer the following questions. Use your textbook and the ideas above.

1. Circle the letter of each condition that makes exploring the ocean difficult.
   a. The ocean is very deep.
   b. The water is very cold in the deep ocean.
   c. The pressure in the deep ocean is great.

Ocean Zones

2. Sonar is a system that uses _____ waves to find the distance to an object.

3. Is the following sentence true or false? People only very recently began using the ocean for trade.

_____

Features of the Ocean Floor (pages 134–136)

Key Concept: **If you could travel along the ocean floor, you would see the continental shelf, the continental slope, the abyssal plain, and the mid-ocean ridge.**

- The ocean floor is not a flat, sandy area. It has mountain ranges, deep canyons, and many other features.

- The **continental shelf** is a gently sloping, shallow area at the edge of a continent.

- The **continental slope** is the steep dropoff at the far edge of the continental shelf.

- On the ocean floor, there are both flat areas and mountains. The **abyssal** (uh BIHS ul) **plain** is a smooth, nearly flat region of the ocean floor. The **mid-ocean ridge** is a very long mountain range that winds around Earth. The mid-ocean ridge passes through all of Earth's oceans.

- A **trench** is a deep canyon in the ocean floor.

Answer the following questions. Use your textbook and the ideas above.

4. Is the following sentence true or false? The ocean floor is a sandy, flat area. _____

Ocean Zones

5. Draw a line from each feature to its description.

Feature	Description

Feature

continental shelf

continental slope

abyssal plain

mid-ocean ridge

trench

Description

a. a smooth, nearly flat region of the ocean floor

b. a very long mountain range that winds around Earth

c. a gently sloping, shallow area at the edge of a continent

d. a deep canyon in the ocean floor

e. the steep dropoff at the far edge of the continental shelf

6. The picture below shows features of the ocean floor, including the mid-ocean ridge, the abyssal plain, the continental slope, and the continental shelf.

a. Make an X on the continental shelf.

b. Draw a circle around the mid-ocean ridge.

Ocean Zones

Movements of the Ocean Floor (pages 136–139)

Key Concept: Plate movements have shaped many of the most dramatic features of Earth, both on land and under the ocean.

- Earth is made up of layers. Earth's center is called the core. The thin, rocky outer layer is called the crust. The thick layer between the crust and the core is called the mantle.

- Earth's crust is broken into many pieces. The pieces of Earth's crust are called **plates**. Plates are under the continents and under the ocean floor. The plates move very slowly on top of the mantle.

- The movements of Earth's plates have formed the sea floor, trenches, underwater volcanoes, and mountain ranges.

- The mid-ocean ridge is between plates that are moving apart. As the plates move apart, melted rock moves up between the plates. This process is called **seafloor spreading**. Over millions of years, seafloor spreading has formed the ocean floor.

- When plates move into each other, one plate sinks under the other. The sinking plate is pushed inside Earth. This allows the ocean floor to spread out at some places while Earth itself stays the same size.

Answer the following questions. Use your textbook and the ideas above.

7. Is the following sentence true or false? Plates are underneath the continents and underneath the ocean floor. _____

Ocean Zones

8. Read each word in the box. In each sentence below, fill in the correct word or words.

seafloor spreading   plates   ridges

a. The moving apart of the plates at the mid-ocean

ridge is called _____.

b. The pieces of Earth's crust are called

_____.

9. Circle the letter of each sentence that is true about the movements of Earth's plates.

a. Seafloor spreading has produced the ocean floor.

b. The mid-ocean ridge is located in the center of one huge plate.

c. When plates move into each other, one plate sinks under the other.

Ocean Habitats (pages 141–145)

Ocean Zones and Conditions (page 142)

Key Concept: **Ocean zones include the intertidal zone, the neritic zone, and the open-ocean zone.**

- The ocean is divided into three zones: the intertidal zone, the neritic zone, and the open-ocean zone.

- The **intertidal zone** stretches from the line made by the highest tide on shore to the line on the continental shelf where the lowest low tide ends.

- The **neritic zone** goes from the low-tide line to the edge of the continental shelf.

- The **open-ocean zone** is the vast area beyond the edge of the continental shelf.

- Each of the three ocean zones has its own physical conditions. The physical conditions of a zone determine what kinds of organisms live in that zone.

Answer the following questions. Use your textbook and the ideas above.

1. Draw a line from each ocean zone to its location.

Zone	Location
intertidal zone	**a.** the vast area beyond the edge of the continental shelf
neritic zone	**b.** from the low-tide line to the edge of the continental shelf
open-ocean zone	**c.** stretches from the line made by the highest tide on shore to the line on the continental shelf where the lowest low tide ends

2. The picture below shows the three ocean zones. Circle the letter of the neritic zone.

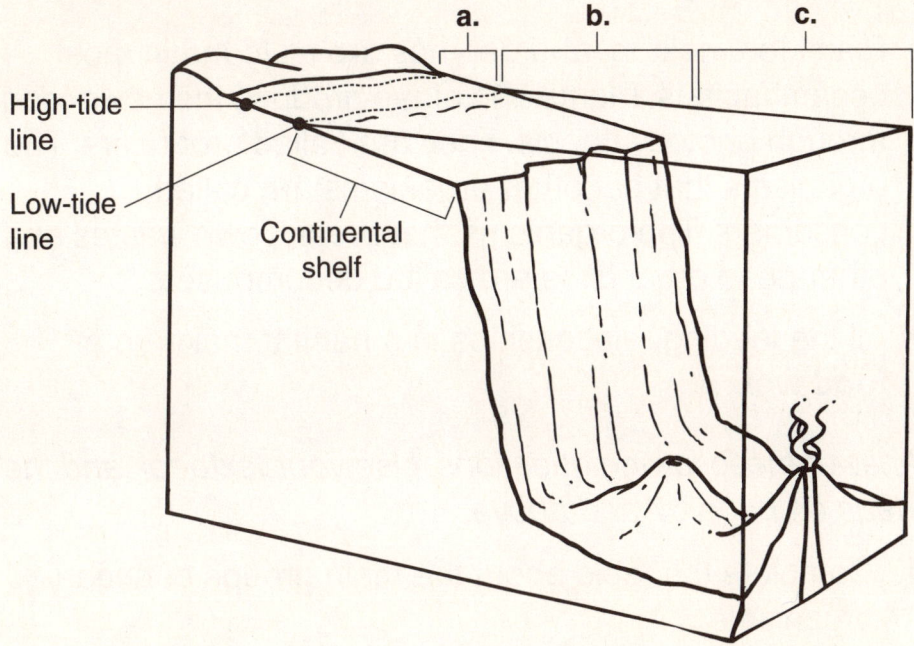

3. Is the following sentence true or false? The physical conditions of an ocean zone determine what kinds of organisms live in that zone. _____

Life in the Ocean (pages 143–145)

Key Concept: **Scientists classify marine organisms according to where they live and how they move.**

- There are three main groups of ocean organisms: plankton, nekton, and benthos.

- **Plankton** are tiny organisms that float on the water. Plankton include some kinds of algae, such as diatoms. Plankton also include very tiny fish and shellfish.

- **Nekton** are animals that can swim throughout the water column. Nekton include fishes, whales, seals, and squid.

- **Benthos** are organisms that live on the ocean floor. Benthos include crabs, sea stars, lobsters, and sponges.

- Plantkton, nekton, and benthos are all found in most ocean habitats. Plants and algae produce their own food through photosynthesis. They are called producers. The organisms that eat other organisms are called consumers. The organisms that break down wastes and other dead organisms are called decomposers.

- All the feeding relationships in a habitat make up a **food web**.

Answer the following questions. Use your textbook and the ideas on page 67 and above.

4. Complete the table about the main groups of ocean organisms.

Main Groups of Ocean Organisms	
Group of Ocean Organisms	**Description**
a. _____	tiny organisms that float on the water
b. _____	animals that can swim throughout the water column
c. _____	organisms that live on the ocean floor

5. All the feeding relationships in a habitat make up a(an)

_____.

Name _____ Date _____ Class _____

Intertidal Zone (pages 146–149)

Rocky Shores (pages 146–147)

Key Concept: **Organisms that live in the rocky intertidal zone must be able to tolerate the pounding of the waves and changes in both salinity and temperature. They must also withstand periods of being underwater and periods of being exposed to the air.**

- Organisms that live in the intertidal zone must be able to live in harsh conditions. The waves pound. The temperature often changes. The salinity of the water can change, too.

- Rocky shores are found along both coasts of the United States. At the top of the rocks is the spray zone. This is where a spray hits from the ocean smashing against rocks below. Some organisms live on the rocks below the spray zone, including barnacles and limpets.

- When the tide goes out, some water stays in large puddles among the rocks. These large puddles are called tide pools. Organisms that can live in tide pools include sea stars, sea urchins, and sea anemones.

Answer the following questions. Use your textbook and the ideas above.

1. Circle the letter of each condition that an organism in the intertidal zone must be able to live with.

    a. The waves pound.

    b. The temperature always stays the same.

    c. The salinity of the water can change.

2. Is the following sentence true or false? When the tide goes out, some water stays in tide pools among the rocks. _____

3. Circle the letter of where the spray zone is found.
   a. in the tide pools
   b. at the top of the rocks
   c. at the bottom of the rocks.

Where River Meets Ocean (pages 148–149)

Key Concept: **Along the coasts of the United States, most wetlands are either mangrove forests or salt marshes.**

- **Estuaries** are inlets or bays where fresh water from rivers mixes with salt water from the ocean. Estuaries contain brackish water. Brackish water is water that is partly salt water and partly fresh water.

- Mangrove forests are found in southern Florida and along the Gulf of Mexico. Mangroves are short trees that grow in brackish water. Mangrove forests protect the land by breaking the waves and the wind that comes off the ocean. Many young animals are raised in mangrove forests.

- A salt marsh is made up of mud, animal and plant matter, and nutrients. Cordgrass is the most common plant in salt marshes. Within a salt marsh, many crabs, shrimp, and oysters hatch and grow before going to the open ocean. When the tide goes out, many big birds walk across the mud hunting for food.

- The rivers that flow into estuaries can carry many pollutants. Organisms that live in estuaries can be harmed by these pollutants.

Ocean Zones

Answer the following questions. Use your textbook and the ideas on page 70.

4. An inlet or bay where fresh water from a river mixes with salt water from the ocean is called a(an)

   _____.

5. Complete the concept map about coastal wetlands.

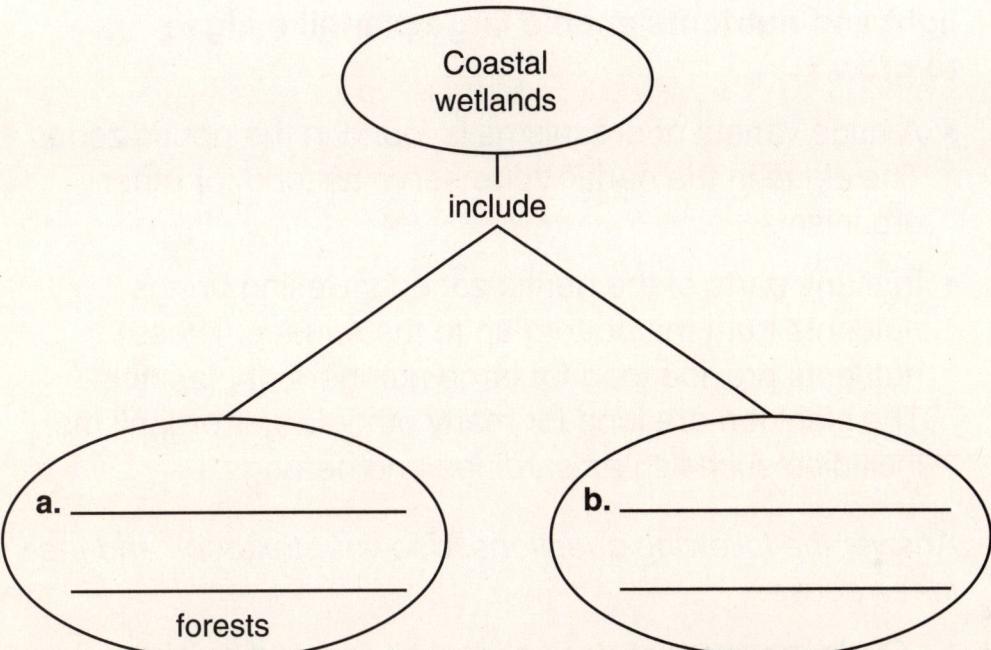

Neritic Zone and Open Ocean (pages 150–157)

Conditions in the Neritic Zone (page 151)

Key Concept: The shallow water over the continental shelf receives sunlight and a steady supply of nutrients washed from the land into the ocean. The light and nutrients enable large plantlike algae to grow.

- A huge variety of organisms is found in the neritic zone. The algae in the neritic zone serve as food for other organisms.

- In many parts of the neritic zone, upwelling brings nutrients from the bottom up to the surface. These nutrients provide food for large numbers of plankton. The plankton are food for many other larger organisms, including such fish as sardines and herrings.

Answer the following questions. Use your textbook and the ideas above.

1. Circle the letter of each sentence that is true about conditions in the neritic zone.

    a. Nutrients from upwelling provide food for large numbers of plankton.

    b. Plankton are food for many other larger organisms.

    c. Organisms in the neritic zone must live in total darkness.

2. Is the following sentence true or false? Nutrients that provide food for plankton are brought to the ocean surface by upwelling. _____

Coral Reefs (pages 152–153)

Key Concept: **Coral reefs can form only in shallow, tropical ocean waters.**

- Coral reefs are found in the neritic zone. Coral reefs are formed by colonies of tiny coral animals. Each coral animal produces a hard structure that surrounds its body. After the coral animal dies, the structure remains. Over many years, a reef is built.

- Algae live in the bodies of coral animals. Algae need warm water and sunlight. As a result, coral reefs grow where the water is shallow.

- An **atoll** is a ring-shaped coral reef that surrounds a shallow pool of water. An atoll begins as a fringing reef that surrounds an island. Over time, the island sinks, and the reef grows upward. Finally, the reef surrounds a shallow pool called a lagoon.

- Many animals live in and around a coral reef. Coral-reef animals include octopuses, lobsters, shrimp, and fishes of all colors.

- Human activities can harm coral reefs. Boat anchors break up reefs. Divers can break off pieces of reefs. Pollution can harm coral reefs. Water that is too warm can destroy coral reefs. Now, people try to protect coral reefs. Many reef areas have been protected as marine parks.

Answer the following questions. Use your textbook and the ideas above.

3. Is the following sentence true or false? Many animals live in and around a coral reef. _____

Ocean Zones

4. The pictures show steps in the formation of an atoll. But the steps are not in the correct order. Number the pictures 1 to 3 to show the correct order of how an atoll forms.

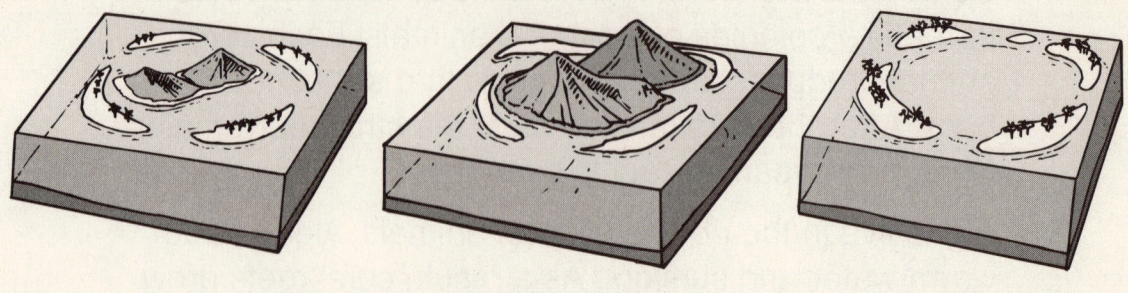

_____   _____   _____

Life in a Kelp Forest (page 154)

***Key Concept:* Kelp forests grow in cold neritic waters where the ocean has a rocky floor.**

• Kelp are large, heavy algae. A giant kelp can grow up to 30 meters long. Kelp have little bulbs called air bladders that keep them upright in water.

• The kelp use sunlight to produce their own food. Kelp forests provide habitats for many organisms, including sea slugs and snails.

Answer the following questions. Use your textbook and the ideas above.

5. Kelp are large, heavy _____.

6. Is the following sentence true or false? Kelp forests grow in cold neritic waters. _____

Conditions in the Open Ocean (pages 155–157)

Key Concept: The open ocean differs from the neritic zone in two important ways. First, only a small part of the open ocean receives sunlight. Second, the water has fewer nutrients.

- The open ocean has fewer organisms than the neritic zone. This is because the open ocean receives less sunlight and has fewer nutrients.

- Few organisms live in the deep zone of the water column. It is so cold and dark there. Many deep-sea fishes produce their own light. **Bioluminescence** is when living things produce light.

- There is one environment in the deep zone where many different organisms live. A **hydrothermal vent** is a place where hot water rises out of cracks in the ocean floor. Many organisms live around hydrothermal vents.

Answer the following questions. Use your textbook and the ideas above.

7. Draw a line from each term to its meaning.

Term	Meaning
bioluminescence	**a.** when living things produce light
hydrothermal vent	**b.** a place where hot water rises out of cracks in the ocean floor

8. Circle the letter of each way that the open ocean differs from the neritic zone.

    a. The open ocean has more organisms than the neritic zone.

    b. The water of the open ocean has fewer nutrients.

    c. Only a small part of the open ocean gets sunlight.

Resources From the Ocean

(pages 158–164)

Living Resources (pages 159–160)

Key Concept: People depend heavily on fishes and other ocean organisms for food. Ocean organisms also provide materials that are used in products such as detergents and paints.

- Many kinds of fish are caught to be eaten. Most fishes are caught near coasts or in areas of upwelling.

- Overfishing causes the number of fish to go down. New tools have helped people catch large numbers of fish quickly. Sometimes the fish are caught faster than they can reproduce. The fish in an area can become hard to find.

- **Aquaculture** is the farming of saltwater and freshwater organisms. In aquaculture, people build the right environment to raise organisms. Oysters, shrimp, and salmon have been successfully raised.

- Algae are used in products such as detergents, shampoos, and paints.

Answer the following questions. Use your textbook and the ideas above.

1. The farming of saltwater and freshwater organisms is called _____.

2. Is the following sentence true or false? Algae are used in some detergents. _____

Ocean Zones

3. Complete the flowchart about how fish become scarce.

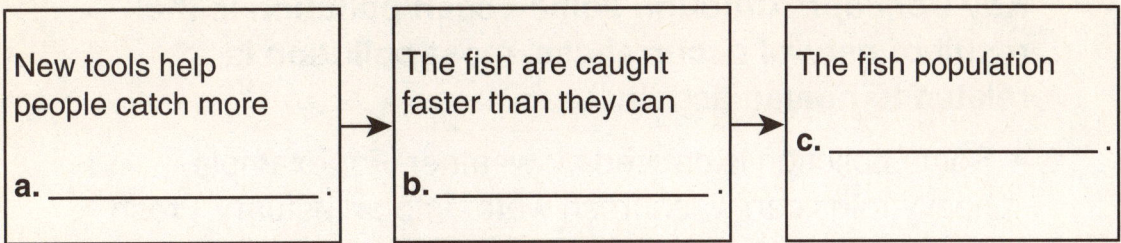

New tools help people catch more	The fish are caught faster than they can	The fish population
a. _____ .	b. _____ .	c. _____ .

Nonliving Resources (pages 161–162)

Key Concept: **Some nonliving ocean resources include water, fuels, and minerals.**

- Fresh water can be made from salt water by desalination.

- The remains of ancient ocean organisms are the source of oil and natural gas underneath the ocean floor.

- Minerals are solid substances that can come from the ground and from water.

- People mine minerals from the ocean floor. Diamonds and gold are mined from sand deposits. Some metals, such as manganese, can be found on the ocean floor. A **nodule** (NAHJ ool) is a black lump formed when a metal builds up around a piece of shell. Nodules are gathered from the deep ocean.

Answer the following questions. Use your textbook and the ideas above.

4. A black lump formed when a metal builds up around a

piece of shell is a(an) _____.

5. Circle the letter of each nonliving ocean resource.

   a. fish

   b. minerals

   c. fresh water

Ocean Pollution (pages 162–164)

Key Concept: **Although some ocean pollution is the result of natural occurrences, most pollution is related to human activities.**

- Some pollution is caused by weather. For example, heavy rains can wash fresh water into an estuary. Fresh water lowers the estuary's salinity, and that can kill some ocean organisms.

- Sewage, chemicals, and trash are dumped into ocean waters. Runoff from fields and roads goes into oceans.

- Oil pollution is a major threat to ocean organisms. An oil tanker or an oil platform may leak oil. Oil is harmful to organisms, and many die.

Answer the following questions. Use your textbook and the ideas above.

6. Circle the letter of each sentence that is true about ocean pollution.
   a. Oil pollution is a major threat to ocean organisms.
   b. Some ocean pollution is caused by weather.
   c. Runoff from fields and roads can pollute the ocean.

7. Is the following sentence true or false? Most ocean pollution is related to human activities. _____